M000159925

Starting and Managing
Your Small Business

Based on the Scriptures and Godly Assistance

Norris Christian

ISBN 978-1-64349-050-2 (paperback)
ISBN 978-1-64349-051-9 (digital)

Christian Faith Publishing, Inc.
832 Park Avenue
Meadville, PA 16335
www.christianfaithpublishing.com

Printed in the United States of America

Contents

Acknowledgment

A special thanks to Emma McElvaney Talbert, my college classmate and friend, Anna Irvin, church member, who had faith in me and kept encouraging me to finish my book. Even though it took me many years to complete, they never gave up on me. Emma reviewed a sample of my writing after telling me she could not wait until I was finished with my book so she could read it. They gave me the courage and incentive to complete my book in spite of a major emotional setback.

My late friend Kim Rogers and I entered into a partnership agreement to co-author this book, but we were never able to act on this agreement because of her ongoing illness. This was a total disappointment to me. Kim was a brilliant writer and one of the nicest people I had the pleasure of knowing. It was a definite pleasure working with her. I want to give my thanks to Darryl, her husband, for affording me the opportunity to be her friend and to know her. After the departure of my friend, it was a must that I complete this book. That is what we had envisioned and what I wanted to do for many years. With the help of the Lord, I knew this book could be completed and He would receive the glory.

I want to give my thanks to Barbara Whyte, my lifelong friend, for her efforts in assisting me with procuring a typist. I would also like to thank Elizabeth Swain for the outstanding job of typing the draft to be presented to the publisher.

A very special thank-you to Randolph "Randy" Gray II for the outstanding job he did creating the illustrations. They added volume to my project. Thank you to Tura Jones for proofreading the final copy of my book. Thank you Shannon Drummond Photography, LLC. for taking my photo for the cover page.

Finally, it is with great compassion that I dedicate this book to the memories of Kim Rogers.

5

The Author

In 1974, the Kentucky Commerce Cabinet received a grant from the U.S. Department of Commerce, Office of Minority Enterprise (OMBE) to create an Office of Minority Business Enterprise for the State of Kentucky. The main office was in Frankfort with satellite offices in Lexington and Louisville because these locations had the greater concentrations of African-Americans.

I was hired that same year by the Commerce Cabinet to work in the Louisville office as a business development officer. My primary responsibility was to assist African-Americans in securing SBA Guarantee Loans, to start or expand a small business. After two years of working primarily with the preparation of financial proposals, I was promoted to education and training coordinator. I was given the responsibility of coordinating workshops, seminars, etc., that would enable our clientele to improve their knowledge of owning and running a successful small business. Two years later, I was promoted to the assistant director in charge of the Louisville Office. In 1981, due to administration changes, we lost our grant with the U.S. Department of Commerce and I was transferred to the main office in Frankfort.

Fortunately, the newly created Office of Small Business had a vacancy and I was put in charge of the office. Over the next eighteen years there were numerous changes, but I continued to work with small and minority business clients.

In October of 1999, I was appointed by Governor Paul Patton as director of the Small and Minority Business Division within the Kentucky Cabinet for Economic Development. As with most state agencies, we had a small staff. Our efforts were devoted to providing information and identifying resources that could be utilized by persons interested in starting or expanding an existing business.

During my tenure, as part of the Cabinet's strategic plan, the Small and Minority Division was responsible for developing a resource database that would assist our clients in the preparation of planning to start or expand a business. After researching and compiling data for over two years, and the outstanding assistance of the IT staff, we were able to develop the website. A special thanks goes to Blake Bennett for his hard work in coordinating the development of the Entrepreneur Resource Navigator (ERN).

I retired from the state government on July 31, 2003. Later, I learned ERN was selected as the best website in Kentucky state government and was submitted for national recognition. Although this occurred after my retirement, I am happy to know the ERN came about as a result of my efforts. One of my most proud moments during my tenure was being the recipient of the Ferda Porter Advocacy Award presented by the Kentuckiana Minority Supplier Development Council. The award recognized my progress and success with small and minority businesses throughout Kentucky.

When I retired, I tried to decide how I would use my time. Being an analytical person, I looked back over my past experiences, and I realized that I had spent twenty-nine years working with small and minority businesses and all of my life attending church.

My involvement with my church doesn't end there, I was actively involved in the preparation of the financial proposal for my church, Antioch Missionary Baptist Church. I explained to the committee, that was assisting me, the importance of a detailed proposal. The point I emphasized was that we needed to approach the bankers with historical data, projections, etc., and not with just a Bible in our hand. Furthermore, I wanted them to understand we had to look at this from the bankers' prospective—as a business. Looking back, I like to think what I said was true, but we could have taken the Bible along with the other information.

Prior to becoming a career state employee, I was a claim representative for Travelers Insurance Company for five years. Before I was a claims representative, I taught general mathematics at Jackson

8

Junior High School, now known as Meyzeek Middle School. Although I only taught for three years, I developed an appreciation for the desire to impart and to share knowledge and to help others to grow intellectually. Therefore, the desire to teach still remained.

To satisfy this desire, I decided to consider the idea of helping others to grow spiritually. I pursued this idea by becoming a nine-to-eleven–year-old Sunday School Teacher in the youth department of my church. I did this for twenty years. Later I felt it was time for me to start attending an adult class.

After being in the adult class, our teacher had to give up the position she really loved due to health issues. The members in our class decided we would pick someone from within our class to be the teacher. After some trial runs from some of the class members, I was persuaded to assume that position.

I served in that position, which I truly enjoyed, for approximately six years. In May 2017, I was diagnosed with multiple myeloma. In addition to the cancer, I was dealing with a chronic back condition that had gotten worse. Between the side effects of the chemo and having constant back pain, it became impossible for me to attend church, much less be an effective teacher.

My wife, Naomi, has been an outstanding caregiver. I don't have the words to express my sincere appreciation. When someone does something for you out of love rather than duty, it becomes special. I have also received great support from my family, church members, and old friends. This, along with the grace and mercy of the Almighty, has sustained me as I continue this journey.

Norris Christian

Mission Statement

When the Lord sent his only begotten son to earth, he was sent on a specific mission—"For the Son of Man came to seek and save the lost" (Luke 19:10, NIV).

One of the steps in planning your business is to develop a mission statement. Before developing your mission statement, you have to do some brainstorming to determine what will be your market, what goods or service you will be providing, and what will make your business unique.

Your mission statement will keep you focused as your business grows. The purpose of your business must be your own vision. "... Write the vision and make it plain upon tablets ..." (Hab. 2:2b, NIV). Also, it is worth remembering, "Where there is no vision, the people perish ..." (Prov. 29:18b, KJV).

Introduction

During my career counseling potential and existing entrepreneurs, I participated in many pre-business seminars. To prepare for the seminars, I did a great deal of research. At this point, I would like to share with you some of the information I obtained and still remember.

Why do you want to start or expand your business?

When the participants were asked that question, usually the answer was to make money or to be their own boss.

If you want to make money, you can do that by working for someone. If you have training and skills that are in great demand, you can earn more than a six-figure salary. So, rethink your motive.

If you want to be your own boss, you need to know your customers will become your boss. Remember, "The customer is always right."

So, the question remains. Here are some suggestions for you to consider when you want to start a new business.

1. You have an idea for a product of service that will solve a problem. This is called niche marketing.
2. You have an idea how to improve an existing product or service. The market has not been saturated, and there is room for your business.

However, if you don't want to start a business from scratch, there are other options. You can seek to acquire an existing business. If you decide to acquire an existing business, here are some options:

1. The owner is retiring and wants to sell.
2. The owner dies and the business has to be sold.

3. The owner is going through a divorce and must sell.

Keep in mind these must be businesses with a proven track record.

I would like to assume that you have decided to pursue your dream of owning your own business. So let me tell you why I decided to write this book. The reason I wrote this book is to encourage you by promoting the utilization of biblical scriptures in the creation and management of your own business venture. "All scripture is God-breathed and is useful for teaching, rebuking, correcting and training in righteousness, So that the man of God may be thoroughly equipped for every good work" (2 Tim. 3:16–17, NIV).

By utilizing the scriptures in the development of your business, it will allow you to "do everything in a decent and orderly manner" (1 Cor. 14:40, KJV).

My ultimate objective is to encourage you to manage your own business based on the scriptures.

The Importance of Small Businesses

But Jesus said, "Suffer little children, and forbid not, to come unto me: for of such is the kingdom of heaven."

—Matthew 19:14 (KJV)

Just as little children were important to Jesus, small businesses are vital to our economy. Starting small businesses is like having little children—easy to conceive, but hard to deliver. Speaking of children, I would like to tell you about two exciting moments in my life. One was when I saw my daughter, Christina, for the first time and the excitement of bringing her home. The other time was when my son, Anthony, was born.

As my daughter and son grew, I tried instilling in them the importance of maintaining an open and steadfast relationship with their mother and me. To me this was very important. I realized there would be times when they would not do this. However, I wanted them to believe they could talk to us during the good times and the bad times. Even today, I like to believe they still feel comfortable talking to me about different things that are going on in their lives.

Just as I believe that children should develop a good relationship with their parents. I believe you, as a small business owner, should develop a good relationship with God. "The Lord is my Shepherd" (Ps. 23:1, NIV). By doing this, when hard times come (believe me, they will), you will be able to talk to Him. Through your relationship with God you will develop and grow your business.

As children grow into mature adults, they get married, they have children, and the process continues for generations to come. Likewise, your small business can grow, expand, and become diversified, thereby creating more small businesses. However, there will be growing pains.

As I said when Anthony was born, it was an exciting moment in my life, but it was one of the most painful moments in the life of Tura, his mother. To endure the pains, she kept repeating the 23 Psalm. As your business grows, He will guide you in paths of righteousness (Ps. 23:3a) and you will go through the valley of death, "hard times"; but goodness and mercy will enable you to endure and you will be able to make a contribution to society and our economy.

According to Janean Chun, "The Small Picture," Small Business Success, Volume 15, in an economy that has shaken the confidence of most, one segment still stands firm—small business. Representing more than 99.7% of all employees, and generating three-quarters of net new jobs in the United States, small businesses have been and continue to be major contributors to our nation's economic growth.

If you believe you have been blessed with an idea to start your own business, you should evaluate your personal characteristics to determine if you are likeable to be an entrepreneur.

IDEA

The Lord will provide you with an idea that will solve a problem enabling you to start your business. Keep in mind, the Lord is working through you to help his people. Therefore, don't think you can take all the credit for what happens. Be his vessel and give Him the glory

Entrepreneurial Characteristics

Have you ever wondered, "How do I know I'll be a successful business owner?" While there are no guarantees to being a successful entrepreneur, you must be all of the following:

Risk Taker

When Nehemiah heard about the conditions of Jerusalem, he was so overcome that he cried. Although he was born in captivity and had not seen the city, Nehemiah clearly loved Jerusalem. The walls were in tatters.

Nehemiah was a cupbearer in the king's court; he allowed his distress to show on his face. This was a dangerous action for Nehemiah to take, because the king's servants were expected to always display a cheerful appearance before him. Nehemiah knew the king could execute anyone who displeased him, but Nehemiah had prayed and trusted God. After Nehemiah explained the problem, the king asked him what he wanted (Neh. 2:4, KJV).

As an entrepreneur, you have to be willing to take many risks in developing your business. However, if you have the proper relationship with the Almighty, you will be able to achieve your objectives. Keep in mind Nehemiah always prayed first before acting. The key to Nehemiah's success was his total reliance on God.

Negotiator

After he prayed, he asked for permission to travel to Jerusalem. He also asked the king for letters of safe travel and a letter to Aspen, the king's forest keeper authorizing him to give Nehemiah timber to use in rebuilding the walls.

During the course of day-to-day management of your business, there will be many issues that will be solved based upon your negotiations. Therefore, you need to develop your skills in this area. If you want to be more like Nehemiah, keep in mind he was a man of prayer and tactfulness.

Researcher

Although Nehemiah had received reports that the walls and gates were in ruins, he decided to do an investigation on his own. He went out in the middle of the night without telling anyone what he was doing. Once he had gathered all the facts, he was now ready to share them with the people (Neh. 2:11–16, KJV).

Before you start or expand your business, you have to do your due diligence. All your assumptions must be checked out and verified. This has to be done by you.

Motivator

After seeing the condition of the walls, Nehemiah knew that he would not be able to repair the walls by himself. He had to enlist the help of others. He did this by appealing to their sense of pride and responsibility. He included himself in plans to rebuild the walls. A good leader knows he must include himself as a part of the plan.

When you present your ideas to potential and existing investors, bankers, etc., you must convince them that you are the most important part of this venture. "Then I said to them, 'You see the distress that *we* are in, how Jerusalem lies in waste, and its gates are burned with fire. Come and let *us* build the wall of Jerusalem, that *we* may no longer be a reproach.' And I told them of *the hand of my God* which had been *good upon me*, and also of the king's words that he had spoken to me. So they said, 'Let *us* rise up and build.'

Then they set *their hands* to *this good work*" (Neh. 2:17–18, NKJV; italics mine).

Based on your evaluation and desire to start your own business, now is the time to get started.

Getting Started

To usher in the year 2010, my son Anthony, who is the Minister of Worship, invited me to attend the Watch Night service at Bates Memorial Baptist Church. Dr. F. Bruce Williams preached a dynamic sermon explaining how the Israelites had been freed from captivity in Babylon and were allowed to return to Israel. Many of the Israelites were excited about the possibility of returning to their homeland.

However, in order for the Israelites to return to their homeland, they had to make the long and difficult journey through the wilderness. This would not be an easy task. Not only would it test their endurance, but it would also be a test of their faith. This was the determining factor whether or not they wanted to return to their homeland; did they have the determination to make the journey through the wilderness? Of course many liked the idea but were not willing to make the commitment.

Rev. Williams pointed out that many of us want to be successful but we don't want to go through the wilderness. As I listened to the message, it made me realize many entrepreneurs are like the Israelites. They fantasize about a successful business, but they don't want to do what is necessary to make the business a success.

To make your business a reality, you need to do the following:

- Do extensive research; that's going through the wilderness!
- Develop a detailed business plan; that's going through the wilderness!
- Secure adequate financing; that's going through the wilderness!

- Select a team of professionals—accountants, insurance agents, lawyers and bankers; that's going through the wilderness!
- Plan the grand opening; that's going through the wilderness!

To have a successful business, you have to make sacrifices, work hard, and stay focused—you will have to go through the wilderness. "I will even make a way in the wilderness, and rivers in the deserts. The beast of the fields shall honour me, the dragons and the owls; because I give waters in the wilderness, and rivers in the deserts, to give drink to my people, my chosen." (Isa. 43:b19–20, KJV).

In the end you will achieve your goal and your business venture will be blessed. Just as the Israelites were the chosen, you can be chosen too. "For I will pour water upon him that is thirsty, and floods upon the dry ground: I will pour my spirit upon thy seed, and my blessing upon thine offspring" (Isa. 44:3, KJV).

Keep in mind one of the reasons for creating a small business is to provide a service or product that will solve a problem. If you have the right relationship with the Lord, he will tell you what you should do. Actually, you will become an instrument through which He can carry out his work. At no time should you think that this was achieved by you alone, but you should give Him the glory.

In order to prepare to start your own business, you should do extensive research. Based upon your research, you should be able to determine if there is a market that will support your proposed business.

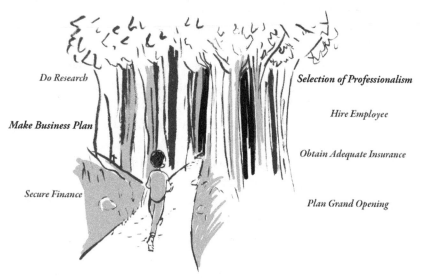

GETTING STARTED

Do Research

Make Business Plan

Secure Finance

Selection of Professionalism

Hire Employee

Obtain Adequate Insurance

Plan Grand Opening

If the Israelites wanted to return to their homeland, they had to go through the wilderness. Likewise, if you want to start your small business, you too have to go through the wilderness.

Market Research

In order to develop a detailed business plan for your business, it is imperative that you do adequate research. "Suppose one of you want to build a tower. Will he not first sit down and estimate the cost to see if he has enough money to complete it? For if he lays the foundation and is not able to finish it, everyone who sees it will ridicule him, saying, 'This fellow began to build and was not able to finish'" (Luke 14:28–29, NIV). You are responsible for doing the research to determine what planning is to be done to make your business venture a reality.

However, the Lord has provided you with an earthly vessel to assist you in developing your plans to start or expand your business. This vessel is known as the Small Business Developmental Center (SBDC). According to the Kentucky SBDC, it is a partnership between the U.S. Small Business Administration (SBA) and typically a local college or university that is designed to help foster small businesses. Small Business Development Centers provide free marketing, financing, and business- related activities to local entrepreneurs. They are found in all states, as well as Washington, DC, Puerto Rico, and U.S. territories.

If you have a burning desire to start your own business, you do not have to do it alone. SBDC consultants will work with you to evaluate your readiness and your business plan idea. Once you have committed to the idea of starting your business, they can provide assistance and guide you in the decision-making processes. The SBDC is the vessel through which the Lord is communicating with you to make your idea a reality.

As a testament to the support of the SBDS, my wife's son Ralph Diaz III started a pipefitting inspection and installation business in

New York. The NYC SBDC assisted Ralph in becoming a Certified Minority Owned Business (MBE). Because of his certification, the state of New York will help Ralph's business because he will be eligible for benefits from New York State. One important aspect of the program is to engage his business in procurement efforts obtained by the New York State Government. Ralph's certification will give him an advantage when marketing his services to state agencies and authorities. He will also have the special access to loan and bonding programs and to programs that provide technical assistance.

Just as the SBDC helped Ralph to develop his business, the same services are available to you. Initially, you may not associate with the SBDC as being sent by God. Believe it. The SBDC is a resource that is provided by the Lord to help you in your journey. I am sure you have heard the expression "The Lord works in mysterious ways." Sometimes you do not recognize a blessing when it is given to you. Ralph recognized his blessing. According to Ralph, because of the outstanding service he received from the SBDC, he believed his business would be a great success.

According to the Kentucky Small Development Center, the easiest way to succeed as a new business is to be thoroughly prepared. Therefore, a considerable amount of research needs to be gathered before you can decide to open a business. Areas that need to be researched include

- target market;
- market trends; and
- competitors.

Contact the SBDC in your area for additional assistance in compiling market research. Remember, the Lord is working through the SBDC to help you along the way. Based on your research, you will do business planning and your business plan will assist you in securing financing for your business.

Business Planning

According to Stefan Topfer, planning is one of the most important parts of running a business, no matter whether it is a large multinational corporation trying to plan an expansion or a small business launching an exciting new product.

It is easy to start a project, but without careful planning, it is like setting off on a journey to an unknown destination without a roadmap. You might manage to make it to your destination eventually, but don't be surprised if you get really lost on the way!

As a small business owner, it is very tempting to neglect planning altogether, especially if you are the only person in the company. After all, planning can be a time-consuming process, and for small business owners, time spent planning is likely to be time when they are not earning any money. But the benefits of good planning will far outweigh any temporary loss of earnings. (February 25, 2011. Topfer, Stefan, CEO of Winweb.com)

Your business plan has a twofold purpose. It is more than a financing device. It is also a management tool. In reality, it is the foundation on which you will build your business. Therefore, in order for your business to prosper and grow, it must be built on a solid rock—idea. "Therefore everyone who hears these words of Mine and acts on them may be compared to a wise man who built his house on the rock" (Matt. 7:24, NASB).

During the life of your business, you will experience many situations that will test your knowledge, patience, leadership, management skills, and faith. However, if you have a developed and detailed business plan, you will be in a better position to face the challenges ahead because you have a solid plan. "And the rain fell, and floods came, and the winds blew and slammed against that house; and yet

26

it did not fall, for it had been founded on the rock" (Matt. 7:25, NASB).

Your business plan will be needed to attract investors, obtain financing, secure insurance coverage, and to assist you in the overall management of the business. "Everyone who hears these words of Mine and does not act on them, will be like a foolish man who built his house on the sand" (Matt. 7:26, NASB).

Business planning is essential. It has been said, "Not planning is planning to fail." Don't be like the foolish man. "The rain fell, and the floods came, and the winds blew and slammed against that house; and it fell—and great was its fall" (Matt. 7:27, NASB). Planning allows you to set goals.

Goals are important and key to success of your business. They can help make your dream a reality. Goals guide you so you can do the things that are important to your success and your biblical teaching.

It is okay to seek help and advice from others; however, your goals should be based upon your research, ideas, and assumptions. Don't let anyone, unless you have a partner, set your goals for you. You will be more likely to reach your goals if they are something you envisioned. Your goals will change as you go through stages of developing your business.

Once you have set your goals, keep focused. Creative thinking can put your goals into your subconscious mind. Once in your mind, you will continue to work toward what is important and necessary for the growth and development of your business. As you move forward with your plans, "Ask the Lord to bless your plans, and you will be successful in carrying them out" (Prov. 13:3).

Speaking of success, how do you measure success? Me, I am a very simple person. To me, being successful means seeing a smile on my family's faces. Regardless of how you define success, the Bible says that if you "take delight in the lord, and He will give you your heart's desire" (Ps. 37:4, NLT). This sounds great, but why is it that this seldom happens?

To make this happen, we must put God first by taking delight in the Lord. Jesus told his disciples that if they would "live for Him and make the Kingdom of God their primary concern" (Matt. 6:33, NLT), everything else necessary for life would be given them as well. This, too, applies to your business. Our problem is that we do not know the meaning of true success.

FOUNDATION

A building is no stronger than its foundation. It will enable the building to withstand years of exposure to the weather and other situations. Likewise, your business plan is the foundation for your business.

Write your business plan

Your business plan is the foundation of your business. Learn how to write a business plan quickly and efficiently with a business plan template.

Business plans help you run your business

A good business plan guides you through each stage of starting and managing your business. You use your business plan as a roadmap for how to structure, run, and grow your new business. It's a way to think through the key elements of your business.

Business plans can help you get funding or bring on new business partners. Investors want to be confident they'll see a return on their investment. Your business plan is the tool you'll use to convince people that working with you, or investing in your company, is a smart choice.

There is no right or wrong way to write a business plan. What's important is that your plan meets your needs.

Source: https://www.sba.gov./business-guide/plan/writeyourbusinessplan

Be Careful with Debt

Although it would be great if you were able to capitalize your small business with personal resource, this may not be the case. Therefore you may have to go into debt to start your business venture. In the event that you make the decision to obtain financing through a loan, keep in mind not to overextend yourself financially.

If you create too much debt, creditors will be the owners and you will be just an employee. Also, if you borrow money for your business, every effort should be made to ensure the loan is paid in full. "The rich ruleth over the poor, and the borrower is servant to the lender" (Prov. 22:7, KJV). "Owe no man anything; but to love one another: for he that loveth another hath fulfilled the law" (Rom. 13:8, KJV).

Business Angels/Investors

Financing your business may be one of the most difficult obstacles to overcome when starting your own business. You probably think if you have excellent credit you will be able to obtain financing from your banker. I would like to point out, banks are not in the business of making loans for start-ups. Banks are not risk takers. If you have never been in business, you do not have a proven track record. Even though you may have a great idea, you have no proof the business can take on a major loan and repay from the profits of the business. Banks have to protect their depositors' investments. Banks want collateral! If you are starting out, it is very likely you do not have sufficient assets that can be used to collateralize the loan.

Unless you have personal savings or equity in your home that you are willing to use, your options are limited. Most small businesses are started from personal savings. I do not recommend this, but many are started with credit cards. You do have the option of taking on an investor, sometimes referred to as a "business angel."

A "business angel" is someone who is interested in an equity position in your business along with a role in the overall management of your business. Eventually, you can buy out the business angel's interest at some future date. On the other hand, you may be able to find an investor who is only interested in a return of his/her investment. As you look for a business angel or an investor, keep in mind the parable of the good sower (Matt. 13:3–8).

In order to find the right business angel, you have to do your due diligence. You have to be sure you have the same values and goals. There has to be the right "chemistry mix." You are the sower— sowing your idea for a new business. "... Behold, the sower went out to sow" (Matt. 13:3b, NASB).

30

A word of caution, as you seek out investors—sowing your seeds—protect your idea. Don't allow someone to take your idea. "And as he sowed, some seeds fell beside the road, and the birds came and ate them up" (Matt. 13:4, NASB).

There are several types of investors with different motives. You will meet what I call "fast talkers" who will appear to be interested in your business at the beginning, but when the growing pains start, they are nowhere to be found. "Others fell on the rock place, where they did not have much soil; and immediately they sprang up, because they had no depth of soil" (Matt. 13:5, NASB).

On the other hand, you may have someone who wants to grow your business too fast and are not able to handle the growing pains. "But when the sun had risen, they were scorched; and because they had no roots, they withered away" (Matt. 13:6, NASB).

There may be some investors, who just want to take over your business because they see the potentials. "Others fell among the thorns, and the thorns came up and choked them out" (Matt. 13:7, NASB).

However, when you find the right investors, it will be with someone who is not only willing to invest in your business but is interested in taking an active part in taking your business to the next level. "And others fell on the good soil and yielded a crop, some a hundredfold, some sixty, and some thirty" (Matt. 13:8, NASB).

Check your local listings for the following shows:

Shark Tank is an American reality television series that premiered on August 9, 2009, on ABC. The show is a franchise of the international format Dragons' Den, which originated in Japan in 2001. *Shark Tank* shows aspiring entrepreneur-contestants as they make business presentations to a panel of "shark" investors, who then choose whether to invest (Wikipedia).

The Profit. When Marcus Lemonis isn't running his multibillion-dollar company, Camping World, he goes on the hunt for struggling businesses that are desperate for cash and ripe for a deal. In each one-hour episode of *The Profit*, Lemonis makes an offer that's impossible to refuse—his cash for a piece of the business and a percentage of the profits. And once inside these companies, he'll do almost anything to save the business and make himself a profit; even if it means firing the president, promoting the secretary, or doing the work himself (CNBC Make It).

FINDING A BUSINESS ANGEL
-Matt. 13: 3-8

When you sow your ideas, some of them will fall by the way-side; someone will want to grow your business too fast. Some of your investors will want to take your idea because of its potential, but someone will be totally interested and want to be involved with the overall management.

Naming Your Business

"And I say also unto thee, that thou art Peter, and upon this rock I will build my church; and the gates of hell shall not prevail against it" (Matt. 16:18, KJV). In the Bible, a name is much more than an identifier as it tends to be in our culture. Personal names (and even place names) were formed from words that had their own meanings. Thus, the people of the Bible were very conscious of the meaning of names. They believed there was a vital connection between the name and the person it identified. A name should somehow represent the nature of the person.

This means that the naming of a baby was very important in the Bible. In choosing a name, the parents could reflect the circumstances of the child's birth, their own feelings, their gratitude to God, their hopes and prayers for the child, and their commitment of the child to God (Nelson's New Illustrated Bible Dictionary).

Jesus changes Simon's name to Peter, "the rock," because he was the first disciple to have solid faith in Him.

Selecting a name for your business should be taken seriously. It should be representing what your business is about. Your name says who you are. Your name is the rock on which you will build your business—your reputation depends on it.

When I started my part-time business engaging in preparing income tax returns with my partner, Floyd Taylor, we decided to name the business Christian & Taylor Tax Service. Whenever we told anyone the name of business, they knew immediately what service we provided and who we were. When it came necessary for us to dissolve our partnership, I changed the name to Christian Tax Service LLC.

33

In our times of greatest joy and our deepest need, the name we cling to is Jesus. He will never leave us, and His love will not fail (McCasland, David).

**YOUR COMPANY NAME IS AS IMPORTANT AS
YOUR COMPANY FUNCTION**

*It's the first thing
customers see*

*It sums up everything
a company is about*

*It's your unique take on
an industry*

To put it simply, it's more than just a name; it's the identity of an entire brand. It deserves time and attention, and when handled properly, it'll change a business forever.

Your company name plays a monumental role in a brand's growth and perception, meaning it can completely make or break a company.

Adam Fridman NAMING YOUR COMPANY 9HTTPS://WWW..INC.COM/NAMING

Insurance
(The Full Armor)

One Sunday in June 2016, while attending the morning church service at my home church, Antioch Missionary Baptist, Rev. Woodrow McElvaney preached on the subject "Putting on God's Armor." It was a dynamic sermon and very informative and thought-provoking. During the sermon, he explained how each part of the physical armor represented a spiritual characteristic.

Paraphrasing an article that was found on http://www.bibleinfo.com/en/questions/armor-of-god, I would like to take a look at each piece of this spiritual armor and see how it can enable you to be victorious as an entrepreneur in your battle against the hardships you will encounter as you attempt to operate the day-to-day activities of your business.

1. **Belt of truth** (Eph. 6:14)

   The belt holding together the full armor of God, is your personal commitment to truth—to live a life that is upright, transparent, and without deceit. Integrity and honesty are vital to your entrepreneurial life. Your customers, vendors, and the general public should know that they can depend on you to be a person of truth and principle.

2. **Breastplate of righteousness** (Eph. 6:14)

   The breastplate covers the heart and shields it and the other vital organs. The Bible says, "Keep your heart with all diligence, for out of it spring the issues of Life" (Prov. 4:23, KJV). It protects you against all of the false accusations and charges.

It is Christ's righteousness—not our own righteousness—that covers and protects us.

3. **Shoes of the gospel** (Eph. 6:15)

Hardships and emergencies are obstacles you will encounter in your path, but in Jesus's strength, you can walk forward, following your Lord, obeying Him, and advancing your business.

4. **Shield of faith** (Eph. 6:16)

When you are attacked with doubts, the shield of faith turns aside the blow. When temptation comes, faith keeps you steadfast in following Jesus. You are able to withstand all the hardships that come your way because you know whom you have believed (2 Tim. 3:12). This faith is something that comes from within you. It is God's gift to you. He gives you a measure of faith (Rom. 12:3). Then as you walk with Him, that faith grows and develops until it becomes a shield protecting you and allowing you to enjoy a victorious business venture.

5. **Helmet of Salvation** (Eph. 6:17)

The helmet protects the head—perhaps the most vital part of the body since it is the seat of thought and the mind. When you have a sure knowledge of your salvation, you will not be moved by evil deceptions.

6. **Sword of the spirit** (Eph. 6:17)

The sword of the spirit is the only weapon of offense listed in the armor of God. All the other parts are defensive in nature. God's Word—the Bible—is described as "living and powerful, and sharper than any two-edged sword" (Heb. 4:12). Jesus used this weapon when Satan tempted Him in the wilderness. To each of Satan's efforts to lead Him into sin, Jesus replied, "it is written …" and proceeded to quote Scripture to destroy Satan's temptation. That is why it is so important that you study the Bible and become familiar with its truth and its power.

The sword of God's Word both protects you and destroys your enemy—the devil and his temptation.

7. **Prayer** (Eph. 6:18)

Although prayer is not one of the pieces of the whole armor of God, yet Paul closes his list by saying, "Praying always with all prayer and supplication in the Spirit" (Eph. 6:18a, KJV). Even when you are clothed with the armor of God, you need to bathe it all in prayer. Prayer brings you into communion and fellowship with God so that His armor can protect you.

8. **How do you put on the whole armor of God?**

It isn't as difficult as you might think. All the pieces of the armor are found in a relationship with Jesus. Paul said it like this: "But on the Lord Jesus Christ" (Rom. 13:14a, KJV). When you give yourself to Jesus and "put on" His righteousness, you are clothed in the whole armor of God.

"Therefore put on the full armor of God, so that when the day of evil comes, you may be able to stand your ground ..." (Eph. 6:13b, NIV).

As I sat there listening to his message, I began to think about how you as an entrepreneur must be prepared to face evil when it comes your way in the form of accidents, natural disasters, and financial problems, just to name a few. One of the best ways to protect your business, and yourself, is through adequate insurance coverage. To accomplish this, you need the advice of a reputable insurance agent who specializes in providing insurance coverage for your type of business.

I spent a great deal of time and research on this section. I strongly believe having that adequate insurance protection is vital to the operation of a successful business.

During my career with state government, I provided counseling to existing and potential entrepreneurs on the types of insurance coverage as a part of asset management. This counseling was based on five years' experience with Travelers Insurance Companies as a claims representative. I learned that many small businesses were destroyed because they did not have the adequate and/or proper insurance coverage.

INSURANCE

Life Insurance

Liability Insurance

Helmet Protect the Head

Workers's Compensation

Breastplate of Righteusness

Sword of the Spirit

Key Man Insurance

Shield of Faith

Flood Insurance

Auto Insurance

Fire Insurance

Truth

Business Interruption Insurance

Disability Insurance

Shoes of the Gospel

Having the proper insurance coverage for your type of business is your full coat of armor. It will protect you from losses caused by accidents, natural disasters, crimes etc.

Adequate insurance is key to the success of your business.
-BUSINESS OWNER'S TOOLKIT

Dealing with Business Regulations

As a career employee of state government working with small business owners, I became aware of the many business regulations that were imposed upon them. Although these regulations were somewhat burdensome, small business owners were expected to be in compliance with those regulations that were related to their particular industries.

Let everyone be subject to the governing authorities, for there is no authority except that which God has established. The authorities that exist have been established by God. Consequently, whosoever rebels against the authority is rebelling against what God has instituted, and those who do so will bring judgment on themselves. For rulers hold no terror for those who do right, but for those who do wrong. Do you want to be free from fear of the one in authority? Then do what is right and you will be commended. For the one in authority is God's servant for your good. But if you do wrong, be afraid, for rulers do not bear the sword for no reason. They are God's servants, agents of wrath to bring punishment on the wrongdoer. Therefore, it is necessary to submit to the authorities, not only because of possible punishment but also as a matter of conscience. This is also why you pay taxes, for authorities are God's servants, who give their full time to governing. (Rom. 13: 1–6, NIV)

As a small business owner, you will be expected to be aware of the regulations that are domain to your business venture. If you fail to comply, you put your business in jeopardy of substantial fines or possible closure.

Remember the following scriptures:

> Obey your leaders and submit to their authority. They keep watch over you as men who must give an account. Obey them so that their work will be a joy, not a burden, for that would be of no advantage to you. (Heb. 13:17, NIV)
>
> These, then, are the things you should teach, Encourage and rebuke with all authority, Do not let anyone despise you. (Titus 2:15, NIV)
>
> But avoid foolish controversies and genealogies and arguments and quarrels about the law, because these are unprofitable and useless. (Titus 3:9, NIV)
>
> Remind the people to be subject to rulers and authorities, to be obedient, to be ready to do whatever is good. To slander no one, to be peaceable and considerate, and to show true humility toward all men. (Titus 3:1–2, NIV)

Employees

In order for your business to grow and mature into a successful enterprise, you have to surround yourself with good and productive personnel.

The type of service and/or product you produce will be determined by standards you instill in your employees. Your employees, human resources, are one of the greatest assets of your business. Therefore, you must make a concerted effort to hire and maintain talented, committed, and loyal employees. You are like the good shepherd watching over his flock.

Like a good shepherd, as an employer, you should be interested in the well-being and professional development of your employee. "The good shepherd lays down his life for the sheep" (John 10:11b, NASB). If you show your employees that you appreciate them as individuals, they will become loyal employees even during hard times. Likewise, "he will not be like the hired hand when he sees the wolf coming, he abandons the sheep and runs away. Then the wolf attacks the flock and scatters it. The man runs away because he is a hired hand and cares nothing for the sheep" (John 10:12–13, NIV).

You must develop a good working relationship with your employees. "I am the good shepherd; I know my sheep and my sheep know me" (John 10:14, NIV).

You must provide good leadership and share your vision with them. You are a team. "My sheep hear My voice, and I know them, and they follow me" (John 10:27, KJV).

One of the ways to maintain good employees is to let them know they are appreciated, "For the scripture saith, Thou Shall not muzzle the ox that treadeth out the corn. And, the labourer is worthy of his reward" (1 Tim. 5:18 KJV).

41

When an employee does an outstanding job or presents an idea that will improve your business operations, he/she should be recognized and rewarded. "His lord said unto him, 'Well done, good and faithful servant, thou hast been faithful over a few things, I will make thee ruler over many things, enter thou into the joy of the Lord'" (Matt. 25:23–29, KJV).

The next two articles will help you understand why you need a "people strategy" and why employee training is worth the time and investment that you put into it.

Why Every Entrepreneur Needs to Develop a "People Strategy"

If you have people working for you, you need an effective "people strategy." Here are some key points you should begin to consider:

- **Think Strategically**

  Because people issues are integral to the success of your business, you need to develop, communicate and enforce a specific set of policies and practices that reflect your vision. These guidelines should reflect your core values, your company's mission, and your standards of acceptable behavior. They will become an integral part of your operations manual, defining how your company is perceived by others when you are not available to deal with customers or clients yourself. Before you can expect your employees to interpret your vision, you must instill in them the essence of what your business is all about.

- **How HR Practices Affect Your Business**

  Without specific HR guidelines in place, you may end up spending unproductive and frustrating hours dealing with people issues instead of focusing on moving your business forward. As well, you are at greater risk for litigation. Human nature being what it is, employees will test limits and make up their own creative answers to different workplace situations.

EMPLOYEES

Remember- Your employees are the greatest assets of your business.

"...having compassion one for another, love as brethren, be pitiful, be courteous."
(1 Peter 3: 8)

- **Synchronize Your Business Plan and Your People Plan**

  Connect your people strategy with your business strategy. If you run a restaurant and you plan on opening three more establishments (your business plan) and have experienced problems hiring cooks, you might want to consider hiring some apprentice cooks (people plan) before you expand.

  How will your business mission and values align with your hiring process? For example, if excellent customer service is a value you hold dear, how will you recruit people who have demonstrated this value in previous jobs elsewhere?

  Policy development is essential if others are to interpret your vision on your behalf. Be consistent so your subordinates will know how to proceed.

- **Reward and Recognize Performance**

  Your reward and recognition programs must be coordinated. If productivity and efficiency are hallmarks of your business's competitive environment, how will your R&R system

43

recognize and reward behavior that supports this aspect of your business?

Your performance management system might need a tune-up. For example, if you have identified safety as a key component for your business's success, what training will you provide employees so they are properly equipped to work safely?

- **Define Your "Culture"**

  Culture can be defined as the culmination of the day-to-day behavior of a group of individuals. As your business functions on a routine basis, a culture will be created—but will it be the culture you want? By coordinating your business and people plans effectively, and by recognizing your own role as a leader, you will be better able to shape the culture to take the direction you want.

- **Learn to Delegate**

  Entrepreneurs sometimes have a hard time letting go of tasks and responsibilities. As your business grows, learning to delegate will allow both you and your employees to use time effectively and focus your efforts appropriately.

- **Use go2HR as a Resource**

  It takes a tremendous amount of thought and work to develop good HR practices, because there are myriad components to a comprehensive people strategy. They include

  o understanding your legal obligations as an employer,
  o observing occupational health and safety standards,
  o hiring the right people,
  o creating an employee handbook that explains company policies and practices,
  o developing job descriptions that will help you hire the right staff and give each of them a clear understanding of their roles and responsibilities,
  o implementing on-the-job training,

44

o knowing how to conduct performance reviews and give constructive criticism, and

o learning how to promote from within or enhance the skills of existing staff when new opportunities arise within your company.

Employee Training Is Worth the Investment

Staff training is essential for specific purposes related to your business. You may require new workers to undertake instruction in first aid, food handling, or a new booking system. Incorporating training that develops employees toward long-term career goals can also promote greater job satisfaction. A more satisfied employee is likely to stay longer and be more productive while on your team.

- **The Cost of Turnover**

A recent survey indicates that 40 percent of employees who receive poor job training leave their positions within the first year. They cite the lack of skills training and development as the principal reason for moving on.

Consider the cost of turnover. With one fewer worker, your company's productivity slips. Sales decline. Your current staff members are required to work more hours. Morale may suffer. To find a replacement, you spend time screening and interviewing applicants. Once you hire someone, you need to train that person. The cost of staff turnover adds up. Figures vary, but it can cost as much as $2,500, depending on the position, to replace a frontline employee. That is a hefty price to pay for not training staff.

- **Other Benefits of Training**

Despite the initial monetary costs, staff training pays back your investment. Here are just some of the reasons to take on development initiatives:

45

o   Training helps your business run better. Trained employees will be better equipped to handle customer inquiries, make a sale, or use computer systems.

o   Training is a recruiting tool. Today's young workers want more than a paycheck. They are geared toward seeking employment that allows them to learn new skills. You are more likely to attract and keep good employees if you can offer development opportunities.

o   Training promotes job satisfaction. Nurturing employees to develop more rounded skill sets will help them contribute to the company. The more engaged and involved they are in working for your success, the better your rewards.

o   Training is a retention tool, instilling loyalty and commitment from good workers. Staff looking for the next challenge will be more likely to stay if you offer ways for them to learn and grow while at your company. Don't give them a reason to move on by letting them stagnate once they've mastered initial tasks.

o   Training adds flexibility and efficiency. You can cross-train employees to be capable in more than one aspect of the business. Teach them to be competent in sales, customer service, administration, and operations. This will help keep them interested and will be enormously helpful to you when setting schedules or filling in for absences. Cross-training also fosters team spirit, as employees appreciate the challenges faced by coworkers.

o   Training is essential for knowledge transfer. It's very important to share knowledge among your staff. If only one person has special skills, you'll have a tough time recouping their knowledge if they suddenly leave the company. Spread knowledge around—it's like diversifying your investments.

o   Training gives seasonal workers a reason to return. Let seasonal employees know there are more ways than one to contribute. Instead of hiring someone new, offer them a chance to learn new skills and benefit from their experience.

Learning and upgrading employee skills makes business sense. It starts from day one and becomes successive as your employees grow. Granted, it may take some time to see a return on your investment, but the long-term gains associated with employee training make a difference. The short-term expense of a training program ensures that you keep qualified and productive workers who will help your company succeed. That's an investment you can take to the bank.

Related Information:

Training & Development (https://www.go2hr.ca/article-category/training-development)

Return on Investment (https://www.go2hr.ca/article-category/training-development/return-investment)

This article may be republished for non-commercial purposes subject to the provisions of the **Website Use Agreement**. To republish this article, you must include the following notice along with the article: "Copyright © 2017 go2 Tourism HR Society. All Rights Reserved. Republished under license."

TRAINING

Encourage your employees to attend classes, workshops, seminars and conferences to improve their knowledge and skills. Not only will they benefit from doing this, but your business will too.

Taxes

As I have mentioned, I have many years of experience in income tax preparation and tax planning. As a result of this experience, I am aware of the hardships you may encounter in meeting your tax obligations. However, failing to pay taxes that are due can be one of the reasons for your business venture to fail.

To avoid this situation, I suggest you utilize a good bookkeeping and accounting system and maintain a good relationship with your tax preparer or accountant.

In spite of the fact that you may not like paying taxes, this is something that you have to accept as a small business owner. Believe it or not, there are benefits for paying taxes. Taxation for the support of the state first appeared among the Hebrews during the reign of Solomon. Before this, Saul and David had supported their government chiefly from the tribute of subject nations and from loot gained in battle (2 Sam. 8:2–10, Spiritual Harvest Edition).

Matthew was one of the tax officials (Matt. 9:9, KJV), and Jesus is said to have kept company with such officials (Matt. 9:9–10; Mark 2:15–17; Luke 5:29–32, KJV). When asked by the Pharisees whether or not it was lawful to pay taxes to Caesar, Jesus replied, "Render therefore unto Caesar the things that are to Caesar the things are Caesar's and unto God the things that are God's," i.e., the laws of the state are to be obeyed (Matt. 22:17–21; Mark 12:13–17; Luke 20:22–25, KJV). Paul said that taxes should be paid to the state (Rom. 13:6–7 Illustrated Dictionary & Concordance of the Bible).

TAXES

Individual Income Tax

Local Income Tax

Unemployment Insurance.

Corporate Tax

Corporate Tax

Federal Income Tax

State Income Tax

Self-Employment Tax

Sales Tax

Meeting your tax obligations is imperative for the survival of your business. Failing to pay your taxes when due can be the destruction of your business. Bottom line, pay all taxes, registrations and licenses when due.

Dealing with Difficult Employees

Managing employees can be a frustrating experience if your employees become uncooperative and difficult.

When I was the director of Small & Minority Business Divisions, I participated in the Governor's Minority Management Trainee Program to become a Certified Public Manager. To successfully complete this program, I had to complete three hundred hours of classroom activities and complete two written projects.

One of the classes dealt with dealing with difficult employees. I enrolled in this class with the expectation I would be given a quick solution on how to deal with employees who were creating problems in the workplace. Instead, I was introduced to the four personality types.

For the sake of clarity, I would like to briefly explain the four personality types. The four personality types are the A personality which includes people who are very organized and want to be in charge. They are not necessarily detail-oriented but are considered perfectionists. B personality individuals are fast-paced and energetic. They, like C personality type, are detail-oriented and rely on logic and rationale when making decisions. The D personality is for people who have an easygoing pace with work and life in general (hiresuccess.com).

To effectively deal with these various types, you have to recognize that opposite personalities can complement one another. Therefore, they should be allowed to work together. If you are interested in these types of personalities, I suggest you do additional research in this area. This information was presented to whet your whistle.

You may not be in a position to be able to match the appropriate personality types with each other. Therefore, keep in mind the following:

Finally, be ye all of one mind having compassion one of another, love as brethren, be pitiful, be courteous. Not rendering evil for evil, or railing for railing; but contrariwise blessing, knowing that ye are thereunto called, that ye should inherit a blessing. (1 Pet. 3:8–9, KJV)

Who so rewarded evil for good, evil shall not depart from his house. (Prov. 17:13, KJV)

Moreover, as for me, far be it from me that I should sin against the LORD by ceasing to pray for you; but I will instruct you in the good and right way. (1 Sam. 12:23, NASB)

DIFFICULT EMPLOYEES

Type A Personality

Type B Personality

Type C Personality

Type D Personality

Many employees have difficulty in working together because of their personalities. Understanding the different types of personalities will enable you to improve or to maintain a favorable work environment It may be a good practice to have your employees take a personality test.

Dealing with difficult employees is never fun. Nonetheless, it is part of your responsibility. A deliberate approach to navigating these awkward situations will help you succeed.

Source: www.thebalance.com

Delegation

As owner of your business, you are responsible for what happens. The buck stops with you, the owner, but you don't have to do everything yourself. You are responsible for determining what must be done to make your business run smoothly on a day-to-day basis. Once you decide what those tasks are, you select the tasks that have to be done by you and the tasks that can be done by someone else—delegate. Delegation means you assign someone a task that is ultimately your responsibility. You may refuse to delegate because you feel no one can do it like you do or the other person may do it better than you. Believe it or not, there is a person in the Bible who had the same problem. It was Moses.

I am sure you recall how Moses told his father-in-law, Jethro, how he would sit alone and all the people stand before him from morning until evening. And he would decide who was right and who was wrong in all arguments (Exod. 18:14–16, KJV). Jethro realized this was not a good thing; therefore, he told Moses, "You're going to wear yourself out! Then, what will happen to people?" (Exod. 18:17, KJV). Likewise, if you try to do everything yourself, you will not be able to continue to run your business. So, what will happen to it? To avoid this situation, you must learn to delegate.

And Moses chose able men out of all Israel, and made them heads over the people, rulers of thousands, rulers of hundred, rulers of fifties, and rulers of tens. And they judged the people at all seasons: the hard cases they brought unto Moses, but every small matter they judged themselves. And Moses let his father-in-law depart: and he went his way into his own land. (Exod. 18:25–27)

Delegating can provide you with the freedom on planning for the future of your business. When delegating, you must decide: (1)

53

what to delegate, (2) to choose the right person for the task, and (3) to give them the freedom to complete the task.

DELEGATING

Being a business owner does not mean that you have to do everything by yourself. So, what do you do? You use your staff by assigning certain tasks to certain employees based upon their ability to complete them to your satisfaction. This is delegating.

Mentoring for Small Businesses

I have always liked the idea of traveling—visiting relatives and seeing new places. Since my retirement, I have been blessed with the ability to take some nice trips.

In my early years of marriage, my traveling budget was somewhat limited. However, I was able to take my family on vacation every summer. Because my funds were limited, it was necessary for me to do some driving during the vacation.

There were times when I knew where I wanted to take my family, but I did not know how to get there. So I would go to AAA for help in planning my trip. AAA gave me a detailed map. I was also given information about road construction, and places to see and to eat. All of the information gave me confidence that I could get to my destination. Even if the person working for AAA had not been to the place(s) we discussed, I was given everything I needed to have a successful trip.

I realize if you take a trip today, you probably would use your GPS instead of contacting AAA. It doesn't matter which resource you use, the point is you need assistance in order to make your intentions a reality.

As you start or continue your journey of entrepreneurship, I suggest you seek advice from someone who has already made this journey. We will call this person a mentor. Your mentor can let you know what to anticipate as you travel along your journey (venture).

You will need assistance from others who have an ultimate knowledge of how business works. You may try to get that information from business books and classes. While these can be helpful on your own, it is more helpful alongside business mentoring. In a business mentoring relationship, a seasoned business owner meets with a new or potential business owner one-on-one to give advice and boost morale ("Top 10 Benefits of Mentoring" by Miranda Morley).

Advice

The biggest benefit of having a business mentor is having someone you can ask questions and get advice.

Perspective

Business mentors can help you look at problems and situations from perspectives that you would not have thought of on your own.

Improving Skills

Mentors are not like advisers and consultants, who care only about the business venture. Instead, business mentors help you develop your business skills.

Venting

Owning a business can be stressful and frustrating. As a business owner, you'll often need to vent with someone you trust.

Networking

Business mentors can put you in touch with the contacts that can help you make your business more successful. The more networking you do, the more people you meet.

Methods and Strategies

In addition to simply giving advice and helping improve your personal business skills, business mentors can prepare you with a library of methods and strategies that you can pull from throughout your career as a business owner.

Long-Lasting Relationship

Although some mentor-mentee relationships are short-lived, if you hit it off with your mentor, you can foster a long-lasting relationship through which you and your mentor can continue to collaborate for the rest of your career.

Confidence

Knowing that you have a credible mentor to turn to can give you confidence when facing difficult business situations.

Encouragement

Starting a business is difficult, many business owners face challenges early in the process.

Benefits for Mentors

Mentees are not the only people who benefit from business mentoring. Business mentors also experience benefits thanks to collaborative learning. It is my professional opinion that all small business owners should have a mentor. Therefore, I felt it was necessary to include a section of mentoring.

> The way of a fool seems right to him, but a wise man listens to advice. (Prov. 12:15, NIV)
>
> A wise son heeds his father's instruction, but a mocker does not listen to rebuke. (Prov. 13:10, NASB - Study Bible)
>
> He who scorns instruction will pay for it, but he who respects a command is rewarded. (Prov. 13:13, NIV)
>
> Every Prudent man acts out of knowledge, but a fool exposes his folly. (Prov. 13:16, NIV)

Without counsel purposes are disappointed: but in the multitude of counsellors they are established. (Prov. 15:22, KJV - Guidance)

Train up a child in the way he should go: and when he is old, he will not depart from it. (Prov. 22:6, KJV)

Where no counsel is, the people fall, but in the multitude of counsellors there is safety. (Prov. 11:14, KJV)

A wise man will hear, and will increase learning; and a man of understanding shall attain unto wise counsels. (Prov. 1:5, KJV)

Give instruction to a wise man and he will be still wiser, Teach a righteous man and he will increase his learning. The fear of the LORD is the beginning of wisdom, And the knowledge of the Holy One is understanding. (Prov. 9:9–10, KJV)

Apply thine heart unto instruction, and thine ears to the words of knowledge. (Prov. 23:12, KJV)

MENTORING

A Mentor gives advice

Allows you to vent

Gives you perspective

Provides Networking

Long-lasting Relationship

Gives you Confidence

Having someone who has experience in a business similar to yours can be a great resource. This entrepreneur can help you in many situations because he/she has been through them. This entrepeneur is not your competitor but your mentor.

Testimony

From Vision to Victory—This was the Antioch Missionary Baptist Church of Louisville, KY, Inc. slogan for its 1995–1998 Capital Campaign.

The late Rev. Curtis Crawford Jr. had the vision of building a new church for the members of Antioch. Considering the size of the membership, many thought this was impossible. However, the Lord looked favorably upon Rev. Crawford's vision.

On the first Sunday of June 2002, Antioch moved from a small church at the corners of Wilson and Dumesnil into a new church costing over $1,500,000 on seven acres at 3315 Dixie Highway.

After receiving his blessing, Rev. Crawford always started his testimony with "To God be the glory." Just as God blessed Rev. Crawford's dream, He too will do the same for you, and you too can say, "To God be the glory."

My Favorite Song

When I was growing up with my late twin brother, Dorris, we spent a great deal of time with our younger sister, Myra. Even though she was only four years older than us, we called her our baby sister and she took very good care of us.

Sometimes we would do things that would get us in trouble or place us in a strange place. From time to time we would become frightened and seek comfort from her. When we were scared we would say, "Hold our hand, baby sister."

I'm happy to say my sister is still here but not near. Although, today she cannot physically comfort me by holding my hand, I have been able to find comfort in a song that is my favorite. As I listen to the words in this song, I am assured that I may not know about tomorrow and what may happen, but I know who holds my hand!

The spiritual connection between the Lord and me is much greater than the physical and emotional connection that existed between my sister and me. This connection made me a much stronger person! I'm sure as you proceed on your entrepreneurial journey you will travel through some low valleys. During these times you can find great relief in singing praises to the Lord or just listening to some great spirituals.

I would like to share with you an article written by Crystal McDowell for Hear It First (http://hearitfirst.com). The article is entitled "10 Bible Verses About Singing." However, I only selected two verses.

Sing of what God has done.

"Sing to him, sing praise to him: tell of all his wonderful acts" (Ps. 105:2, NIV).

61

God has done and will continue to do great things in the lives of those who love Him. Our immediate response to Him is lifting up grateful hands and singing a song of praise. Singing allows us the opportunity to speak out about what He has done: broken chains of darkness, forgiven sin, and restored strength to those who are weak.

Sing in times of trouble.

"About midnight Paul and Silas were praying and singing hymns to God, and the other prisoners were listening to them" (Acts 16:25, NIV). Singing in the darkest moments of our lives seems strange. However, it's what God's people should do when we are struggling in literal or emotional prisons. We sing our way free from the bondages of fear and anxiety—in doing so, our faith is strengthened to press forward another day.

Just as the Lord heard Paul and Silas during their hard times, surely He will hear you during your period of trouble and difficulty.

Although I do not sing, I truly love listening to good gospel music. In the baptist church, music is a major part of the worship service. Over the years, I have heard many hymns; I have two favorites. As you develop your business, I am sure they will sustain you. During your difficult times, you don't have to worry about tomorrow- Because I Know Who Holds My Hand.
And you will make it in your business; You can believe this-Because He Lives, I Can Face Tomorrow.

Prayer for Business Success

Lord God,

Thank you for the opportunity to run this business.
I trust in your wisdom as I seek to work hard to make it secure and prosperous.
May good practice be the cornerstone of everything I do.
Come reveal new opening and areas for expansion and development.
May this business grow and flourish, creating great opportunity and provision for all those involved.

In the name of Jesus,
Amen.
(www.lords-prayer-words.com)